Smooshed
nose

Wrinkles

Stubby tail

15
in

Slobbery
tongue

Drool

Short legs

26in

evanahrendtbooks@gmail.com

Published in the United States by Evan Ahrendt LLC

ISBN: 978-1-7366086-0-9

For more information or to book an event, visit our website:

www.evanahrendt.com

Paperback

Looking down at our planet way
out in space,
there is a house you may notice
that looks out of place.

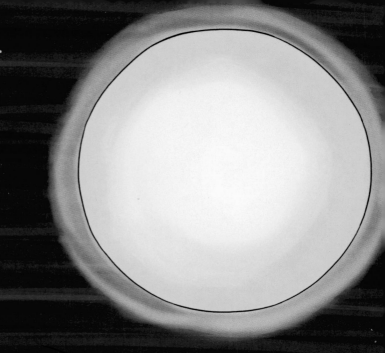

No matter where you observe, this house looks quite
average, but there is someone inside that possesses
great courage.

Here lives Sir Watson,
sworn knight of the land,

Sir Watson once knighted
by a true king and queen,

traveled back many centuries
in his own time machine.

Let's head now to where it all begins.
We haven't much time so strap yourself in.

PRESS TO RELEASE

Silly flamingo, not like that.

Are you ready? Great! Now let's check on Watson.
If he hasn't had dinner, proceed with CAUTION.

Phew! Watson's all snuggled up in his bed,
awaiting his owner to make sure he's fed.

WHOA! Look at the time, it's getting sooooo LATE!
There is only so long Watson is willing to wait.

Watson's owner, Phil, is nowhere to be found.
He can be rather forgetful if he's
at the playground.

Maybe he's off getting
his daily **balloons**,

or possibly fell asleep
watching Sunday cartoons.

Then suddenly, out of nowhere, the floor begins to open, and everything around him is **pulled,** **stretched** or broken.

Watson follows right behind
down through the floor,
his bed is no bed at least not
anymore.

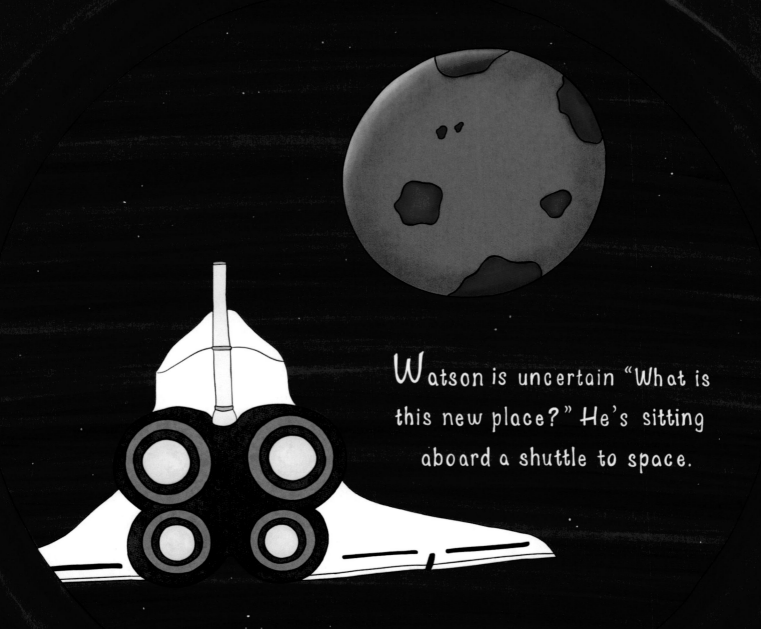

Watson is uncertain "What is this new place?" He's sitting aboard a shuttle to space.

His mission is obvious. Watson's run out of food. It's now up to him at this high altitude.

He turns on the scanner and

aims down at a planet.

Results turn up negative

only basalt rock and granite.

Onto the
next planet
and if needed, the next.

Watson stays optimistic but

is rather

perplexed.

Feeling very frustrated, almost calling it quits, Watson sniffs something familiar and has to admit.

There is food somewhere close
as he picks up a scent,
leaps from the shuttle and begins the
descent.

Watson spacewalks around to find a
MOUNTAIN OF FOOD!
Jumping astroid to astroid, now in a much
better mood.

His tummy will soon be so happy and full. He's going to need a

much,

much,

much

bigger bowl.

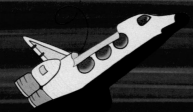

He stuffs every pillowcase, old hat and old shoe.
He packs every last morsel then howls,
"Thank yooooou!"

Headed back home,
Watson is thrilled,
"I've got enough food
to keep me fulfilled."

Watson turns the ignition, but the engine won't start.

This doesn't look good; the shuttle is falling apart.

Watson, now in danger, emergency lights
flash, drifts straight for a planet
"ALERT-ALERT-SHIPS-GOING-TO-CRASH!"

Into Mars surface,
      the shuttle hits
                    HARD!

Watson is ejected,
        landing safe in
    Frank's yard.

Franks Junk Yard that is, which is rather

GIGANTIC.

Frank lives here with Hank;
they are Mars' mechanics.

They return to the shuttle and quickly get it repaired,
Watson's so thankful he offers to share.

Goodbye Watson!

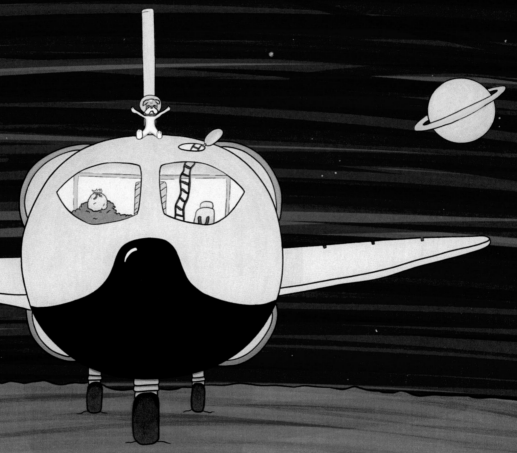

He hops in his shuttle, ready for flight, turns the ignition and the thrusters ignite.

Watson can't wait to finally be home.

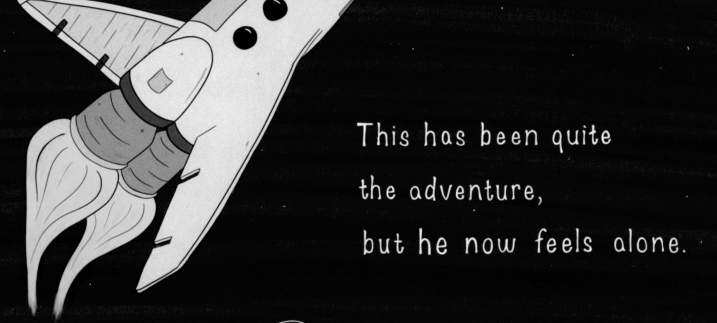

This has been quite the adventure, but he now feels alone.

Before Watson knows it, he's back in his bed.
Was this all just a dream? He feels full and quite fed.

We'll never truly know if Watson made it to space, but one thing's for sure, he's back in the right place.

The End.

This book is dedicated to my daughter Lucille and our lovable companion,

WATSON

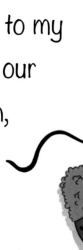

Author's Note

I have always wanted to write and illustrate a children's book, and Watson helped me to accomplish that. This is my very first book and I am so thrilled to share it with you. I hope it becomes a family favorite. Make sure to keep an eye out for more adventures of Watson and his travels.

-E.A.

Made in the USA
Columbia, SC
17 August 2021